Contents

2	Finding information	24	Fact or opinion?
4	Vocabulary in context	26	Supporting sentences
6	Reading in detail	28	Sentence types
8	Finding the main idea	30	Direct speech
10	Summarising the main idea	32	Reading play scripts
12	Looking for clues	34	Reading non-fiction
14	Interesting words	36	Reading poetry
16	Using quotations	38	Predicting
18	Looking at layout	40	Active reading
20	Reading aloud	42	Quick test
22	Imagery	44	Explorer's logbook
		46	Answers

Introduction

If you are wild about learning and wild about animals – this book is for you!

It will take you on a wild adventure, where you will practise key reading comprehension skills and explore the amazing world of animals living across the continent of Asia.

Each reading comprehension topic is introduced in a clear and simple way with lots of interesting activities to complete so that you can practise what you have learned.

Alongside every topic you will uncover fascinating facts about some of the animals living in Asia.

Asia covers a huge area that reaches almost halfway round the Earth and is home to some of the world's most interesting and unusual animals.

When you have completed each topic, record the animals that you have seen and the skills that you have learned in the explorer's logbook on pages 44–45.

Good luck, explorer!

Rachel Grant

Finding information

Sometimes when you are reading, you need to be like a detective and **find the details**! To do this, read the text carefully. Focus on the specific words you want to find. Then read the words next to them to understand the detail.

WILD FACT

Siberian tigers are the largest big cats in the world.

FACT FILE

Animal:	Siberian tiger
Habitat:	South east Russia and northern China
Weight:	180 to 320 kg
Lifespan:	10 to 15 years
Diet:	Elk, bears, boars and deer

WILD FACT

Unlike other tigers, Siberian tigers have thick manes to keep them warm.

Task 1 Read the headline and find the details to answer the questions.

Kuzya the Siberian Tiger from Russia Reaches China

a What is the tiger's name? _____

b Where is it from? _____

c Where is it now? _____

Five tigers were released into eastern Russia in May. They had been rescued when they were cubs. Their mothers had been killed by poachers. The tigers were set free with trackers in their collars so that scientists can follow where they go.

Tick the correct word to complete these statements.

a The tiger cubs were ...   rescued ☐   lonely ☐

b Their mothers had been ...   killed ☐   lost ☐

c Their collars had ...   tags ☐   trackers ☐

Task 3 Read the next part of the article and answer the questions.

The adult tigers were ready to go back to the wild. 'We made sure they were fit and healthy before we let them go,' said Dr Romanov. Now one of the tigers, named Kuzya, has crossed into China. He swam across a river to get there. There are about 360 wild tigers in Russia but there are only about 24 in China.

a Who looked after the tiger cubs? _____

b How did Kuzya reach China? _____

c How many tigers are there in Russia? _____

d How many in China? _____

Exploring Further ...

Unscramble the letters in these words to make a new phrase. The first letter of each word has been done for you.

HANDSET FILED IT

F_ _ _ _   T_ _ _   D_ _ _ _ _ _ _

Now pad to pages 44–45 to record what you have learned in your explorer's logbook.

Vocabulary in context

Sometimes when you are reading, you will meet a word that you do not know. Try to work out the **meaning** from the rest of the words in the sentence or paragraph. Then, to check that you have the right meaning, look up the word in a dictionary.

FACT FILE

Animal: Bactrian camel
Habitat: Deserts in Central and East Asia
Weight: 816 kg
Lifespan: Up to 50 years
Diet: Plants

Task 1 Read the sentences and work out what the words in bold mean. Underline the correct meaning.

WILD FACT

The Bactrian camel prefers to eat plants but if it can't find any, it will feed on bones, sandals and even tents!

- Wild Bactrian camels will die out if their **natural** habitats in China are destroyed.

a something that is simple   something that is in nature

- Wild Bactrian camels are so **sensitive** that they will run off if they feel danger approaching from 4 km away.

b quick to feel or notice   having good sense

- Believe it or not, camels can be lovable (if **peculiar**) pets, but you will need lots of space!

c normal   unusual

In this paragraph, what do the underlined words and phrases mean? Choose the best meaning from the box.

Many people have wondered <u>whether</u> camels are better than horses. More than a century ago, camels were used to <u>explore</u> the Australian Outback. Camels are not as easy to ride as horses but they can carry more weight. On the other hand, horses can move more quickly and easily through <u>mountainous</u> areas. Camels prefer flat land. Some people say that camels are easier to train than horses, as they are more <u>intelligent</u>.

if	find	steep	clever

a whether _____   **b** explore _____

c mountainous _____   **d** intelligent _____

Read this story. Look for clues that tell you what the underlined words and phrases mean. Write down the meanings.

In the beginning, the Camel <u>refused</u> to work. This <u>irritated</u> the Dog, the Ox and the Horse, who were sick and tired of doing his work as well as their own. However, when they asked him to work, the Camel would only say, 'HUMPH!' The animals <u>complained</u> to the Boss. 'This Camel is an <u>idle</u> creature and all he says is, 'HUMPH!" So the Boss went to the Camel and asked him to work. The Camel <u>responded</u> with a big 'HUMPH!' – but as he spoke, his back grew a big hump. And that <u>explains</u> how the Camel got his HUMP!

a refused _____   **b** irritated _____

c complained _____   **d** idle _____

e responded _____   **f** explains _____

WILD FACT

The Bactrian camel has two humps, which hold fat as well as water.

Exploring Further ...

Find words in these two pages that have the same meaning as the words below. Write the words in the spaces.

a stay alive _____

b environments _____

c load _____

Now stroll to pages 44–45 to record what you have learned in your explorer's logbook.

5

Reading in detail

Often you will need to read a text more than once to understand the details. Read it once to get a **general idea** of what it is about. Read it again, more carefully, to find the **details**. Asking questions can help you to find the details in a text.

FACT FILE

Animal: Asian elephant
Habitat: Tropical forests and grasslands
Weight: 5000 kg
Lifespan: Up to 60 years
Diet: Grass, leaves and fruit

Task 1 Read this text carefully. Decide whether the statements below are true or false.

Elephants need to drink once a day. They live near water for this reason. Their favourite foods are bananas, sugarcane – and rice! However, in the wild they live on tree bark, roots and leaves. They may spend 19 hours each day looking for food. Their trunks are tremendously powerful but also very sensitive. Elephants can use them to tear down whole tree trunks and also to pick up a single blade of grass!

a Oranges are an elephant's favourite food. _False_

b They live near water. _true_

c They spend 10 hours a day feeding. _False_

d Their trunks are very strong, yet extremely sensitive. _true_

WILD FACT

Elephants have larger brains than any other land mammal.

Task 2   Read this paragraph once to get a general idea of what it is about. Then read it again and answer the questions.

The main threat to Asian elephants is to their habitat. Humans have gradually taken over areas where elephants live. When roads, railways and houses are built, there is less land for the elephants to graze and breed. Elephants need a lot of space.

a What is the general idea of the paragraph?_____

b What have humans done to their habitat?_____

c Name three things that take up the elephants' land. _____

_____

WILD FACT

Even though they are huge, Asian elephants can walk silently!

Task 3   Read this text about elephants then complete the grid.

African elephants have large ears. Asian elephants have small ears. The skin of an African elephant is wrinkled and it has a sloping back. The back of the Asian elephant is flat and its skin is smooth. Male and female African elephants have large tusks. Female Asian elephants do not have tusks at all, and the tusks of males are fairly small.

	Asian elephant	African elephant
ears		
skin		
back		
tusks		

Exploring Further ...

Find these words in the word square.

read   **detail**

idea   **order**

S	P	D	I	L	A
C	O	R	D	E	R
I	R	W	E	N	T
D	E	T	A	I	L
O	A	E	G	P	E
B	D	S	O	L	A

Now stroll to pages 44–45 to record what you have learned in your explorer's logbook.

7

Finding the main idea

Task 1 — Answer these questions.

a How many main ideas will you usually find in one paragraph? _____

b Where in a paragraph is the main idea sentence usually located? _____

_____

c Where is the main idea sentence sometimes found? _____

_____

WILD FACT

The blowfish is also known as the pufferfish because when it senses danger, it can blow itself up to several times its normal size.

FACT FILE

Animal:	Blowfish
Habitat:	Shallow waters and coral reefs
Weight:	5 to 15 kg
Lifespan:	4 to 8 years
Diet:	Shellfish and algae

Task 2 Read this paragraph.

In Japan, blowfish meat is considered a rare and delicious food. The Japanese word for blowfish is fugu and there are about 3800 fugu restaurants in Japan. Fugu must be carefully prepared before eating and it is usually eaten raw. Only highly trained chefs are skilled enough to prepare it. Do not try this at home!

a Underline the sentence that contains the main idea.

b What do the other sentences add to the main idea?

_____

WILD FACT

Each blowfish contains enough poison to kill 30 adults!

Task 3 These two paragraphs contain two different main ideas. Read both paragraphs, then answer the questions.

1. Most people are terrified of blowfish. The blowfish is one of the most poisonous creatures on the planet. Its spikes are so deadly that fishermen will not touch it if they catch one by mistake. There is no antidote to blowfish poison.

2. Most types of blowfish are found in tropical oceans but some live in freshwater. Some are marked with colourful spots and stripes, while others are brown, grey and green. There are more than 100 species of blowfish. The common toadfish is actually a type of blowfish.

a Underline the sentence that contains the main idea in paragraph 1.

b Underline the sentence that contains the main idea in paragraph 2.

c What is the topic of paragraph 1? _____

d What is the topic of paragraph 2? _____

Exploring Further ...

Test your knowledge of blowfish! Write (**T**) true or (**F**) false.

a They can blow themselves up to twice their normal size. _____

b Raw blowfish meat needs careful preparation. _____

c There is a cure if you are poisoned by a blowfish. _____

Now swim to pages 44–45 to record what you have learned in your explorer's logbook.

Summarising the main idea

Sometimes you need to **summarise the main idea** of the texts you read. To do this well you need to focus on the **key words**. A good summary that uses your own words shows that you understand the text.

Ask yourself:

- What is the text <u>mainly</u> about?
- Which key words in the text can I use in my summary?

(Hint: often the key words are the repeated words.)

Task 1   Read the headline and the paragraph and then answer the questions.

WILD BOAR POSES FOR PHOTOS!

A large wild boar was seen in a national park in Singapore. He did not seem to be afraid of humans. Wild boars live in the nearby woods, but they are shy. It is very unusual to see one in a public park.

a   Underline the main idea.

b   Circle the three key words in the box.

shy	boar	seen	photos	park	woods

WILD FACT

Wild boars have two pairs of tusks that grow from their bottom and top lips. The tusks are actually huge teeth!

Task 2 — Read the next paragraph of the story and answer the questions.

'I couldn't believe my eyes when I saw this hairy wild boar coming towards me. I thought perhaps he was looking for food,' said Mrs Ling, who was cycling through the park. 'I stopped and the boar came very close to me. He seemed friendly and not dangerous. I took some photos and he enjoyed the attention. He turned left then right, as if he was posing for the pictures.'

a Circle three key words.

b Use the key words to complete this summary:

As she was cycling through the park, _____

stopped and took _____ of a friendly wild _____.

Task 3 — Read the last paragraph of the story and answer the questions.

Numbers of wild boars have increased in recent years. At one time, boars were thought to be extinct in Singapore. Now they are becoming locals! It is amazing that these wild animals can live near to humans. Now it seems that some wild boars are becoming used to humans. So next time you are cycling through the park, be ready to make a new, hairy friend!

a What is this paragraph mainly about? _____

_____

b Underline three key words you will use in your summary.

c Write your own summary of the paragraph. Use no more than 18 words. Use the information you found in parts **a** and **b**.

_____

_____

Exploring Further ...

Answer the clues. The first letter of each answer makes a new word.

a Their tusks are actually these. _____

b It is ___ to see a wild boar in a park. _____

c Where the story took place. _____

d You need to use these words in your summary. _____

New word: _____

Now charge to pages 44–45 to record what you have learned in your explorer's logbook.

11

Looking for clues

Writers do not always tell readers all the details directly. Often when you are reading, you need to **look for clues** to work out deeper ideas.

First, read the text carefully and look for clues.

Then put the clues together.

Finally, use your own knowledge to work out what the writer is telling you.

WILD FACT

The black giant squirrel is the world's largest squirrel.

Task 1 Read this sentence and then answer the questions.

The grandad admitted to trapping the 'terror' pet squirrel.

a Does the man have children? _____

b Was the squirrel wild or tame? _____

c Is the squirrel alive? _____

d Was the squirrel dangerous? _____

e Who thinks so? _____

f How did you work out the answers? Underline the clues in the sentence.

WILD FACT

The black giant squirrel's huge tail helps it to keep its balance when it leaps from branch to branch.

Task 2   Read the sentence then complete the table.

'When it's hot, their black fur actually keeps them cool,' he explained.

Information	Clue in the text
It is hot	
The creatures have black fur	
He knows about this creature	

Task 3   Read the paragraph carefully and then answer the questions.

Last week I noticed some unwelcome guests in the garden. One sheltered under the dripping leaves. Another confidently stole some nuts. The last one leapt from branch to branch, flicking his huge bushy tail at me. They soon ran off when Bill barked at them.

a Does the writer like the creatures? Which word tells you?

_____

b How many were there in his garden? How do you know?

_____

c What was the weather like? Which words tell you?

_____

d What sort of creatures were they? What makes you think so?

_____

e What sort of animal is Bill? How do you know?

_____

Exploring Further ...

Brainteaser: Use your reading power to work out the answer!

A boy was rushed to the hospital emergency unit. The doctor saw the boy and said, 'I cannot operate on him. He is my son'. The doctor was not the boy's father, so how could that be?

Now leap to pages 44–45 to record what you have learned in your explorer's logbook.

Interesting words

Some words are so common that they can be dull to read. However, good writers choose really **interesting words or phrases** to create **interesting ideas and pictures** for readers. As you read, notice the **effect** of the interesting words. What do they add to the text? How do they make you feel? What do you see or hear when you read them?

WILD FACT

The king cobra is the only snake in the world that builds nests for its eggs.

FACT FILE

Animal:	King cobra
Habitat:	Rainforests and grasslands
Weight:	Up to 10 kg
Lifespan:	20 years
Diet:	Other snakes, lizards, eggs and small mammals

Task 1

Choose an interesting word from the box that you could use instead of each of these common words. Write it next to each word.

cheerfully	sweltering	massive	cried	clamorous	delightful

a said _____

b big _____

c nice _____

d happily _____

e hot _____

f noisy _____

Task 2

A student has underlined four interesting words. What is interesting about them? Complete the table.

It was a <u>sweltering</u> day. 'AH-HA!' cried the cobra. 'I smell a <u>massive</u> lizard coming my way. How delightful! Lunch!' The lizard did not see the cobra's shadow until it was too late. With a <u>clamorous</u> hiss, the cobra <u>cheerfully</u> attacked.

Word	Makes me feel/see/hear
sweltering	
massive	
clamorous	
cheerfully	

Task 3

Read the paragraph and answer the questions.

When a King Cobra feasted on a Lizard

We travelled to the densest part of the forest and spotted a king cobra. This one was more than 3.5 metres long. Then we found a lizard moving across a road. The cobra scented its prey like a keen hunter. King cobras have a rapid, deadly strike. It attacked the lizard and started to swallow it head-first. This majestic snake is one of the most dangerous snakes in Asia.

a Underline FIVE interesting words or phrases in the text.

b What is effective about the words you chose? Think about what the words make you feel, see or hear. Complete these two sentences.

The words _____ and _____ make me feel/see

hear _____. The words _____, _____

and _____ are effective because _____.

Exploring Further ...

Find the words in the word snake. You should find seven words.

_____ _____ _____

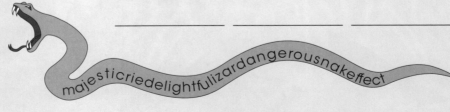

majesticriedelightfulizardangerousnakeffect

_____ _____

Now slither to pages 44–45 to record what you have learned in your explorer's logbook.

Using quotations

When you write about the texts you have read, you need to **explain your ideas**. For example, you might want to explain why a character did something, or describe how something works. To do this, you could use a **quotation** from the text that will support your idea.

A quotation is when you take the exact words from somebody else's writing. We use inverted commas to show what the exact words are, like this:

When it says, 'soak daily', it means that you should put your tortoise in water every day.

FACT FILE

Animal:	Indian star tortoise
Habitat:	Semi-arid forests and grasslands
Weight:	2.5 to 7 kg
Lifespan:	30 to 80 years
Diet:	Leaves and grass

WILD FACT

The shell of the Indian star tortoise is unusual because it has bumps (called pyramids) and star-like patterns.

Task 1 For each sentence, add quotation marks in the correct places.

a The Indian star tortoise has been described as the most beautiful tortoise in the world.

b The phrase star-like describes the pattern on their shells.

c Wildlife protection experts are calling the threat to the tortoises a huge tragedy.

WILD FACT

The shape of the Indian star tortoise's shell helps it to roll back to its feet if it gets turned on its back.

Task 2

Read this email. For each statement below, circle **(T)** true or **(F)** false. Write a quotation to support your answer.

My Indian star tortoise has started to lie in his water bowl. Since getting him three months ago, I have been soaking him daily for 15 minutes before his breakfast, but now he is taking himself off for long soaks every day. Is this normal? His house is not too hot. Thanks so much. Petra

a Petra has owned her tortoise for a long time.   **T   F**

_____

b Petra is worried about her tortoise's behaviour.   **T   F**

_____

c Petra thinks her tortoise's house might be too hot.   **T   F**

_____

Task 3

Read this reply to **Petra's** email then answer the questions using quotations.

Sometimes tortoises dry out too much, so it probably needs to soak more. Some like it if you spray them with warm water. Otherwise, it doesn't seem to be a problem. Best wishes, Tariq

a Why might Petra's tortoise want to soak? _____

b Should Petra spray her tortoise? _____

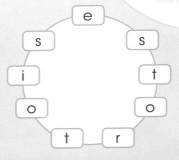

Exploring Further ...

Find the word in the circle. It can start in any position and can go clockwise or anti-clockwise.

_____

Circle letters: e, s, s, i, t, o, o, t, r

Now plod to pages 44–45 to record what you have learned in your explorer's logbook.

Looking at layout

Layout is how a text is **arranged**. In non-fiction, writers use layout to attract readers. They use these special features:

- **Heading** – grabs your attention and make you want to find out more
- **Images** – excite your feelings or emotions
- **Bullet lists** – make details easier to read
- **Capital letters** – are like shouting! They make you pay more attention
- **Words in bold or italic** – give special emphasis to important words

Adopt a Manul Today!

Rare, beautiful and mysterious, but

THREATENED BY FUR TRADERS

It may be the oldest living cat species.
It lives in some of the coldest places on Earth.
ADOPT NOW to SUPPORT this AMAZING and ANCIENT BREED!

For donating just a small amount per month, you will get:

- certificate of adoption
- full-colour photo poster
- gift bag with stickers, bookmarks and more
- information card with fascinating facts

Task 1 Identify the features in the poster. The first letters of each feature have been given to help you.

a h_____

b i_____

c c_____ l_____

d b_____ i_____

w_____

e b_____ l_____

Task 2

Why has the writer made the choices in the poster? Match each feature with the most likely reason. Write the number in the box.

a big image

b bold, italic words

c bullet list

d heading

e capital letters

1 To grab my attention and make me want to find out more.

2 So that I pay more attention.

3 To make me feel emotional about manuls.

4 So that I can read the details quickly.

5 So I know that these are important words.

a [ ]   **b** [ ]   **c** [ ]   **d** [ ]   **e** [ ]

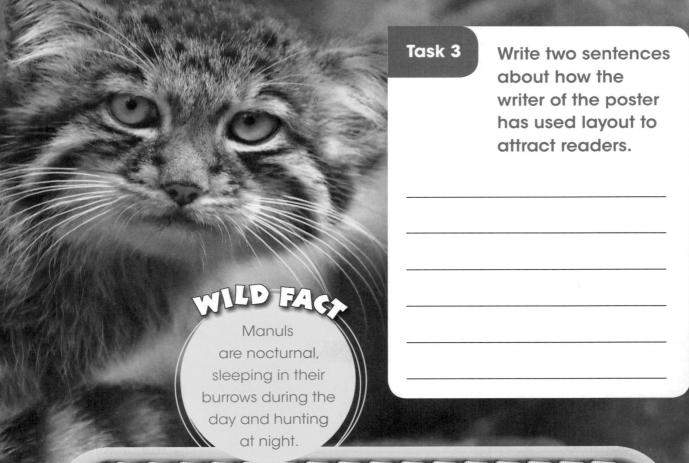

Task 3

Write two sentences about how the writer of the poster has used layout to attract readers.

_____

_____

_____

_____

_____

_____

Exploring Further …

Can you make two new words from all the letters in the word **CATS**?

_____   _____

Now prowl to pages 44–45 to record what you have learned in your explorer's logbook.

Reading aloud

Sometimes it is helpful to **read a text aloud** to help you **understand it better**. When you read aloud, pay extra attention to the punctuation. It gives you clues about how to read the text.

- A comma tells you to pause for a short time.
- A full stop signals a longer pause.
- An exclamation mark shows a feeling. It may be something funny or sad or surprising. Use the tones and volume of your voice to show the feeling.
- A question mark makes it sound like a question. Use your voice to show this.

FACT FILE

Animal:	Atlas moth
Habitat:	Tropical and subtropical dry forests and shrublands
Weight:	25 g
Lifespan:	1 to 2 weeks
Diet:	Adult Atlas moths do not eat anything as they have no mouth

Task 1   Join the punctuation mark to the clue for reading aloud.

a a comma	show the feeling with your voice
b a full stop	pause
c an exclamation mark	make it sound like a question
d a question mark	make a short pause

Task 2   Read this paragraph aloud. Pay extra attention to the punctuation. Then complete the table.

Did you know? Asian moths can look like cobra snakes! When it is threatened, this amazing moth drops to the ground. It flaps the tips of its wings, so that it looks like the head of the deadly cobra snake. This useful camouflage helps the moth to scare off predators. This moth has brains as well as beauty!

Punctuation mark	With my voice, I ...	How did it help the meaning?
question mark	made it sound like a question	made it more interesting
exclamation mark		
comma		
full stop		

Task 3   Read this paragraph aloud. This time, think about the feeling you need to show and how to use your voice to show it.

What am I scared of? I am really, really scared of moths. Their feathery bodies give me the creeps! Sometimes I have a nightmare that my bedroom is full of them, and they're all flying into my face and then they're in my hair! Ugh!

a Circle the feeling the writer wants you to show when you read this aloud.

humour   surprise   fear

b How did you show the feeling? Tick two. Did you make your voice:

higher ☐ lower ☐ louder ☐ softer ☐

c Underline the words in the text that you emphasised to show the feeling.

WILD FACT

The atlas moth has the largest wing surface area of any moth and its wingspan is 25–30 cm.

Exploring Further ...

Solve the anagram. The first letter is already correct.

TRAIL COP   T _ _ _ _ _ _ _

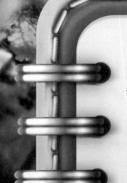

Now flutter to pages 44–45 to record what you have learned in your explorer's logbook.

Imagery

Writers sometimes use **images to create pictures** and feelings in the reader's mind. This is called imagery. To do this, they may use **similes** or **metaphors**.

A simile compares one thing to another thing, using 'like' or 'as'.

Look at these examples:
The fairy bluebird's back is <u>like a blue summer sky</u>.
Its back is <u>as blue as a summer sky</u>.

When one thing is described as if it is another thing, it is called a metaphor.

Look at this example:
It has a blue summer sky on its back.
Here, the bird's back is described as if it is a blue summer sky.

FACT FILE

Animal: Fairy bluebird
Habitat: Forests
Weight: 50 to 100 g
Lifespan: 10 years
Diet: Fruit, flower nectar and insects

WILD FACT

The fairy bluebird has a sweet tooth – its favourite fruit is figs!

Task 1 For each sentence, decide if the writer has used a simile (S) or metaphor (M). Write **S** or **M** in each box.

a Their greenish eggs are perfect, speckled pebbles. ☐

b Young bluebirds are as helpless as newborn babies. ☐

c The fairy bluebird's call is liquid silver, flowing through the air ☐

d The bluebird flies soundlessly, like midnight. ☐

Task 2 Unscramble these sentences to make two similes (S) and two metaphors (M). Then label each one **S** or **M**.

a as delicate/The eggs were/as moonlight.

_____

b soft spring rain./its wings/The beating of/was like/

_____

c flying/ She felt like a / free./ bluebird,

_____

d an enchanted / It holds/ in its wings. / dream

_____

Task 3 Read this text. Find five examples of imagery and decide whether each is a simile or a metaphor. The first one has been done for you.

In the dark forest, the tiny birds are like specks of daylight. As each one takes flight, the butterfly blue of its wings are as bright as sparklers. The nest is a tiny fairy cup of twigs and roots and is half-hidden by moss. Inside are three eggs, nestled together like small clouds.

a *like specks of daylight*   *simile*

b _____   _____

c _____   _____

d _____   _____

e _____   _____

Exploring Further ...

Use the words in the box to complete these well-known sayings.

| kitten   feather   lead   ox |

a As light as a _____.   **b** As strong as an _____.

c As heavy as _____.   **d** As weak as a _____.

Now fly to pages 44–45 to record what you have learned in your explorer's logbook.

23

Fact or opinion?

The gaur is the fourth biggest mammal in the world. Only elephants, rhinos and hippos are bigger!

What is a fact? A **fact** can be proved true.

What is an opinion? An **opinion** is a belief or a feeling. It might be true or false but it cannot be proved.

Look at these examples:

FACT: Another name for the gaurs is Indian bison.

OPINION: Gaurs are really ugly.

FACT FILE

Animal:	Gaur
Habitat:	Forests
Weight:	650 to 1000 kg
Lifespan:	Up to 30 years
Diet:	Grasses, seeds, leaves, flowers and fruit

Task 1   Read these sentences. Label the facts **F** and the opinions **O**.

a It is really funny how their legs have two colours. ☐

b That baby gaur is so cute! ☐

c Gaurs eat grasses in the winter and in the summer they eat fruit. ☐

d Gaurs need to be protected from hunters. ☐

e A gaur uses its horns to attack and its weight to trample its enemies. ☐

Find five facts about gaurs in this paragraph.

The male gaur is black and the female is dark brown in colour. Some are more than two metres high. Measure it! That's really big. I wouldn't like to be on the end of those horns, would you? They are over one metre long. Gaurs are said to be bad-tempered, but I don't believe it. Mind you, they don't look very friendly. They travel in herds and there are about ten animals in each herd.

a Fact 1: _____

b Fact 2: _____

c Fact 3: _____

d Fact 4: _____

e Fact 5: _____

Task 3 Underline **four** facts (in blue pen) and **two** opinions (in red pen) about gaurs in this paragraph.

A male gaur is bigger than a bison, a buffalo or a water buffalo. Even so, gaurs are hunted by tigers, leopards and crocodiles. Tigers are awesome. It is amazing that some gaurs live so long if they are hunted by tigers. Human hunters are the other main threat to gaurs. They are hunted for their meat and their horns.

WILD FACT

The hump on the gaur's shoulders makes it look like a bison from the front, but from the back it looks like a cow.

Exploring Further ...

An anagram of GAUR is RAGU. Use these four letters and add one extra letter to make a five-letter word that means 'to quarrel or disagree'. The first letter is given to help you.

A _ _ _ _ _

Now run to pages 44–45 to record what you have learned in your explorer's logbook.

Supporting sentences

When you read a paragraph, you will notice that there is often one sentence that has the **main idea**. This tells you what the paragraph is **mainly about**. The other sentences in the paragraph give details that **support** the main idea. These are the **supporting sentences**.

Here is an example:

The peacock's tail is magnificent. It has around 200 blue and green feathers. Each green feather has a bright blue 'eye'. The peacock displays its tail in a 'fan' when it wants to attract a mate.

The underlined sentence is the main idea.

Task 1 — Read this paragraph.

A prized pet peacock was stolen last night. The owners realised that it was missing at 10 p.m. They searched the whole property but could not find it. They could not find any evidence that the peacock had been killed by a fox or wolf. They think thieves drove on to the property and took the bird.

a Underline the main idea sentence in this paragraph.

b How many supporting sentences are there?

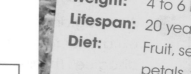

FACT FILE

Animal:	Peacock
Habitat:	Forests and jungle
Weight:	4 to 6 kg
Lifespan:	20 years
Diet:	Fruit, seeds, nuts, petals, worms, ants, lizards and scorpions

Task 2

Read this main idea sentence then decide which one of the options below would NOT be a supporting sentence.

Mr Tallis is heart-broken at losing his bird.

a He bought the blue peacock in 2008.

b He says the peacock, named Mirza, is priceless.

c His feelings are not because of money.

d Mirza is an Indian name and means 'prince'.

e Over the years he has grown very fond of his peacock.

Answer: ☐

WILD FACT

Every year, the peacock drops all its old tail feathers and grows new ones.

Task 3

Read this main idea sentence. Tick four of the options to be supporting sentences.

We have a pair of peacocks in our back garden!

a They arrived in the village two weeks ago. ☐

b They hop from garden to garden. ☐

c Peacocks are beautiful birds but they make an ugly sound. ☐

d We don't know who they belong to, or how to catch them. ☐

e If you know someone who has lost their peacocks, send them over to our village. ☐

WILD FACT

The peacock is one of the largest birds that can fly. Some are more than 1.5 metres long!

Exploring Further ...

Match each clue to the right word. Draw a line to join them up.

a Lions are said to be king of this   peacock

b An insect peacocks like to eat   feather

c Part of a flower   jungle

d A showy bird   ant

e Found in a peacock's tail   petal

Now strut to pages 44–45 to record what you have learned in your explorer's logbook.

Sentence types

Good readers can work out the effect of different types of sentences. If you know the different types, you can understand the writer's meaning. Look at these sentence types:

- A **command** tells you to do something
- A **statement** tells you something
- A **question** asks something
- An **exclamation** shows strong feelings

Task 1   Match the sentence types with the correct definition. Draw a line to join them up.

a Command   expresses an emotion

b Question   gives information

c Statement   asks for an answer

d Exclamation   gives an instruction

WILD FACT

Male birds of paradise are brightly coloured but females are dull in colour to protect them from predators.

WILD FACT

Male birds of paradise will do an amazing dance to show off their incredible feathers when they want to attract a mate.

Task 2 Match the examples with the right sentence types.
Write the number in the box.

1 Young males learn mating dance steps by watching their fathers.

2 Don't use flash when you take pictures of the birds.

3 Wow! I can't believe how beautiful they are!

4 What does a male have to do to attract a female?

a Command ☐   **b** Question ☐

c Statement ☐   **d** Exclamation ☐

Task 3 Read this paragraph. Find one example of each of the
sentence types. Write each one in the correct space.

The king bird of paradise hangs upside down as part of his mating display.
He's a brilliant acrobat! Watch how he swings from side to side. Do you think
he feels dizzy?

Sentence type	Example
Command	
Statement	
Question	
Exclamation	

Exploring Further ...

The words in these sentences have been mixed up.
Put them back in the right order. When you have finished,
identify the type of sentence and write it on the line.

a 'the dancer of the jungle'. / sometimes called / The bird of
paradise is

_____

b gorgeous! / Its tail feathers / are absolutely

_____

**Now dance to pages 44-45 to record what you have
learned in your explorer's logbook.**

29

Direct speech

When you read the words that someone actually said, you will notice that the words spoken are surrounded by inverted commas (`...`), sometimes called speech marks. This is **direct speech**.

'That loris is so cute!' exclaims Patty.

Task 1   **Underline the direct speech in these sentences.**

a   'They look more like teddy bears than wild animals!' said Malia.

b   He said, 'The loris can stay completely still for hours at a time.'

c   'Make a donation to save the loris's habitat!' he urged.

d   'With those thumbs,' he went on, 'they can grip the trees, just like monkeys – or humans!'

e   'They look so furry and cuddly!' said Rakhee.

WILD FACT

Loriș are nocturnal and although they may be slow, they can travel up to 8 km in one night!

FACT FILE

Animal:	Loris
Habitat:	Forests
Weight:	250 g to 2 kg, depending on the species
Lifespan:	15 to 25 years
Diet:	Fruit, plants, nectar and insects

Task 2 Punctuate the paragraph correctly, using speech marks to show what the guide said.

The guide told us some fun facts about the loris. The short second finger on each foot helps it to hold on to branches, he explained. He went on, Its eyes are huge and that means it can see well in the dark. Then he told us, They look cute and furry but they are actually poisonous predators. They cover their teeth before they bite into their enemies!

Task 3 Write down three things the guide told the writer. Use direct speech.

It surprised me to hear that the name loris comes from a Dutch word meaning clown. The guide said it was because of their comical appearance, which makes them very desirable as pets. Unfortunately, he said, loris are hunted and then sold on the streets or in animal markets.

a _____

b _____

c _____

WILD FACT

Like cats, the loris has a light-reflecting layer in its eyes, so it can see in almost total darkness.

Exploring Further ...

These words have all been spelled backwards. Can you work them out?

a SIROL   _____

b SUONOSIOP   _____

c LANRUTCON   _____

Now creep to pages 44–45 to record what you have learned in your explorer's logbook.

31

Reading play scripts

When you read a play script, you need to understand its special layout so you can read it correctly. Look out for:

- **Set directions** – these tell you **WHERE** the play takes place

- **Character names** – these tell you **WHO** is in the play. The name is always followed by a colon (:)

- **Stage directions** – these might tell you **HOW** the characters feel, **HOW** they speak, or **WHAT** they do

- **The lines** – these are the words each character **speaks**

FACT FILE

Animal:	Grey langur
Habitat:	Grasslands and forests of India
Weight:	5 to 18 kg
Lifespan:	20 to 30 years
Diet:	Leaves, fruit, seeds, flowers, insects and roots

Task 1

Read this part of a play script and then answer the questions.

Evening. Three trekkers are climbing a forest trail near Poon Hill.
Rose: (*tired*) Jamil, is it much further? It's so muddy along here!
Jamil: Not far now! Only about two miles.
Suddenly there's a crashing noise from the forest.
Rose: (*shrieking*) What was that?

a Where and when is the play set?

_____

b How many characters are there? _____

c How does Rose feel? _____

d Put a circle around Jamil's lines.

Task 2   Read the next part of the play script, and then answer the questions.

Tara: Probably just a tiger, or an elephant ...
Rose: (*scared*) Look out, look out!
A group of grey monkeys appears in the branches.
Jamil: Relax. They're just curious.
Tara: But what are they? Are they monkeys?
Jamil: They're grey langurs. See how they're hanging
                 from the branches?
Rose: (*smiling*) Awww! They're cute!

a How many characters are there in this part? _____

b How does Rose feel in this part? Circle two:

   nervous   embarrassed   delighted   annoyed   grouchy

Task 3   This is the last part of the play script.
              Read it and then answer the questions.

Jamil: (*laughs*) Well, they're not pets. They're wild animals!
Two big monkeys swing down and land on the floor.
Tara: They've heard you, with those small hairy ears of theirs!
Jamil: (*a bit nervous*) Umm, let's carry on. I don't want to give them
          our sandwiches!
Rose: (*disappointed*) Ohhh! I don't mind feeding the baby one.
          They look like little old men. Look! They're coming closer!
Jamil: (*very urgently*) Guys, if I tell you to run, you need to ... RUN!

a How do Jamil's feelings change in this part?

   From: _____   To: _____

b What stage directions would you give to Tara?   _____

c How does Rose feel about leaving the monkeys? _____

Exploring Further ...

What have you learned about reading play scripts?

   a After the character names there is always a _____

   b Will you find inverted commas around direct speech in a
         play script? _____

   c What shows how the character feels? _____

   **Now swing to pages 44–45 to record what you have
   learned in your explorer's logbook.**

Reading non-fiction

When you read non-fiction texts, it helps to understand what **type of text** you are reading. You can do this by thinking about the writer's **purpose** (reason) for writing. As you read, ask yourself:

- Why has the writer written this text?
  (for example, to persuade, give information or facts, explain how something works or give instructions)

- How has the writer used language to help me understand this text?

Some types of non-fiction texts are: leaflets, newspapers, dictionaries, recipes, advertisements.

Task 1 Draw a line to join the correct purpose to each type of text.

a An advertisement for a mobile phone   gives instructions

b A recipe for biscuits   explains how something works

c A leaflet about zoo animals   persuades

d A user manual for a dishwasher   gives information or facts

Read the text below about the Pangolin Project and then answer the questions.

PROJECT PANGOLIN

Support World Pangolin Day!

This incredible, peaceful creature is under threat and urgently needs our help.

YOU can help us to **SAVE THE PANGOLIN**.
Spread the word about <u>World Pangolin Day</u> on **21st February**

Please take the time to lend a hand!
Ways to help:
- donate
- volunteer
- buy a pangolin T-shirt

WILD FACT

Adult pangolins are covered with very hard scales for protection. Babies are born with soft bodies. Their scales harden two days after they are born.

WILD FACT

Pangolins have extremely long tongues (longer than their bodies!) to catch ants.

a What is the topic? _____

b What is the writer's purpose?

_____

c What type of text is it? _____

d What type of reader is the text aimed at? Circle your choice:

children   wildlife lovers   explorers   gardeners

Exploring Further ...

'Pangolin' is an unusual name. Where did it come from?
Guess which of these is true and tick the box.

a It is named after a saucepan because its hard, shiny scales look like metal. ☐

b It is named after Paul G. Olin, who discovered it in 1776. ☐

c It is named after an old Malayan word for 'roller', because it rolls into a ball when it is attacked. ☐

Now roll to pages 44–45 to record what you have learned in your explorer's logbook.

Reading poetry

Some poems **rhyme** and have a regular beat (**rhythm**). These poems are often called **formal verse**. Some poems do not rhyme and do not seem to follow any pattern or have a strong rhythm. We call these poems **free verse**. Many modern poems are in free verse. They do not seem to follow any 'rules' and they often sound natural, like normal speech.

When you read a poem out loud, or in your head, pay attention to the punctuation marks. These will give you clues to help you understand it.

Task 1 Which of the following would you expect to find in free verse and formal verse? Put a tick in the correct box.

	Free verse	Formal verse
Does not follow any rules		
Often sounds natural, like normal speech		
Usually has a regular rhythm		
Usually rhymes		

Poem A	Poem B
Who scurries, jumps	I know no rules, since
Swings through space,	I'm cooler than most. The fur
A pointed nose	On my tail is in excellent nick.
And furry face?	Leaves and lianas glow in the half-darkness
Who's comical, squirrel-sized,	And night falls –
Brainier than you?	*Life's short: live free.*
The bushy-tailed, button-eyed,	
Asian tree shrew.	

a Which words in poem A are rhyming words? _____

_____

b Is poem A in free verse or formal verse? _____

c How do you know? _____

d Is poem B in free verse or formal verse? _____

e Look again at the two poems. What are some differences between them?
Complete the table.

	Poem A	Poem B
What is it mainly about?		
Who is speaking?		
It makes me feel …		

Exploring Further …

Tree shrew is not an easy name to say out loud. Try it!

Now try this tongue twister: 'The shrewd shrew sold Sarah seven silver fish slices.'

How did you get on? Try to say it five times together, as fast as you can, without making a mistake!

Now scurry to pages 44–45 to record what you have learned in your explorer's logbook.

Predicting

When you are reading, you can use **details** in the text to help you **predict** what might happen.

You might:

- use what you already know to make links between events or characters
- ask questions as you read

You might ask yourself:

What is going to happen next?

How is this going to end?

FACT FILE

Animal: Red-crowned crane
Habitat: Marshes, swamps and lakes
Weight: 7 to 9 kg
Lifespan: 30 to 40 years
Diet: Fish, insects, grasses, rodents, fruit, nuts, leaves and worms

Task 1   Read these titles and predict what you think each text will be about.

a *Legend of the Red-Crane* _____

_____

b *Cranes Past and Present* _____

_____

c *The Crane Mystery* _____

_____

d *How to Fold a Paper Crane* _____

_____

Task 2

Read each part of this fairy story then write what you think will happen next. Cover up the next part until you have written your prediction!

One snowy day, an old man found a crane caught in a trap. 'Oh, you poor thing,' said the man and he helped to free it. The crane flew off over the mountains.

a What will the man do next? _____

_____

The old man went home and told his wife what he'd seen. Suddenly, there was a knock at the door. It was a beautiful young woman dressed all in white. She looked very cold. The old man said, 'Come in and warm yourself by the fire.'

b Who do you think she is? _____

The young woman excelled at weaving and made the softest white cloth the couple had ever seen. However, she did her weaving alone. 'You must never look inside the room when I am weaving,' she said.

c What do you think the couple will do? _____

_____

One day the couple opened the door a little. Inside, they saw a white crane weaving with its bill and its own white feathers to make the cloth. Quietly, they closed the door.

Task 3

How do you think the story ends. Write your prediction.

_____

_____

Exploring Further ...

Find the three-word name of the bird in the word-search grid.

P	C	S	R	G	N	M
C	R	O	W	N	E	D
C	A	P	Y	N	U	L
N	N	E	E	R	W	N
R	E	D	H	G	E	D

Now fly to pages 44–45 to record what you have learned in your explorer's logbook.

39

WILD FACT

The large flying fox is a kind of 'megabat'. It is the world's second largest bat!

If you are reading a tricky text, it may help if you become an **active reader**. Slow down and **ask yourself questions** as you read, to check your understanding. Practise using these 'question' words:

- Who?
- When?
- Why?
- What?
- Where?
- How?

Task 1 — Read this title and answer the questions.

Fun Facts about the World's Widest Bat

a What do you expect the article to be about?

_____

_____

b Write down one question you have about the title.

_____

_____

FACT FILE

Animal: Large flying fox
Habitat: Tropical forests and swamps
Weight: 0.6 to 1.1 kg
Lifespan: 15 years
Diet: Leaves, fruit, nectar, pollen and flowers

WILD FACT

When it rests, the large flying fox hangs upside down from tree branches, with its wings wrapped around its body.

Read this article then read the question. Read the article again. As you read, try to answer the questions.

The large flying fox has a wingspan of over 1.8 metres. It uses those enormous wings to fly up to 60 km in one night in search of food. It has a unique communication system. Scientists have identified that it can make around 30 specific calls. Unfortunately, its population is in significant decline. Its habitat is being destroyed and it is also hunted as a pest.

a What is the main topic? _____

b How big are its wings? _____

c What is special about it? _____

d What does 'in significant decline' mean?
_____

e Who might hunt it? _____

Task 3 Write two questions to help someone to understand this text.

The honour of being the bat with the largest wingspan on the planet goes to the large flying fox. This giant megabat looks like some monster straight out of an 1980s horror movie! Its Latin name is *Pteropus vampyrus*. That second word looks an awful lot like vampire to me. Hmmm! I wonder if human blood is listed on its diet sheet?

a _____

b _____

Exploring Further ...
Complete this crossword about the flying fox.

Across
3. It likes to eat these.
4. It likes to live in these.

Down
1. It hangs upside ___ at rest.
2. It is this kind of bat.
3. It looks like one, but isn't!

Now fly to pages 44–45 to record what you have learned in your explorer's logbook.

Quick test

Now try these questions. Give yourself 1 mark for every correct answer – but only if you answer each part of the question correctly.

1 Read this text and complete the fact file.

The Siberian tiger is the largest of the big cats (306 kg). Unlike lions, tigers live alone. Their striped gold, black and white fur is a camouflage. They do not run great distances but stalk and pounce on their prey.

Fact file: Siberian tiger

a Weight: _____ **b** How they hunt: _____

c Colour: _____

2 Choose the correct meaning from the box for the underlined words.

excite	live	harmful	essential

a A camel's humps help it to <u>survive</u> for a long time without water. _____

b A camel is therefore <u>indispensable</u> to desert travellers. _____

3 Read this text and answer the questions.

An elephant can carry a load of 545 kg and needs 136 kg of food a day. A baby can weigh 90 kg when it is born. Elephants live a long time – up to 70 years.

a What is the general idea? _____

b How much does a baby elephant weigh? _____

4 Underline the main idea in this text.

Every year, some animals migrate (travel) from one region to another. Fish use their sense of smell. Birds use the position of the sun in the sky to find their way. Mammals use their memory.

5 Tick the best summary for the text in Question 4.

a Some animals migrate.

b Different animals migrate in different ways.

6 Read this text. What is Jane's job?

Jane checked her uniform in the mirror and went back to the ward. She checked Mrs Parson's records, and smiled at her. 'Don't worry! Everything's fine,' Jane said.

_____

7 Choose an interesting word from the box that you could use instead of each of these more common words.

fascinating	joyful	substantial	exquisite

a interesting _____

b beautiful _____

8 Add quotation marks in the correct places in this sentence.

Habitat loss has been described as the biggest threat to endangered animals.

9 **Name two features of layout that can help you understand a text.**

a _____

b _____

10 **Read this sentence aloud.**

All animals matter, but some are closer to extinction than others. Read on to discover which ones.

a What does the comma tell you to do? _____

b What should you do when you reach a full stop? _____

11 **Read this example of an image. Is it a simile or is it a metaphor?**

The sun was a huge, red hot air balloon in the sky. _____

12 **Decide whether these sentences are fact (F) or opinion (O).**

a The ostrich is my favourite bird. _____

b The ostrich is the world's largest bird. _____

13 **Underline the supporting sentences in this paragraph.**

Animals that live in cold parts of the world survive in different ways. Arctic foxes have fur that changes from brown to white. Penguins tuck their flippers close to their bodies to stay warm. Large mammals, such as bears, hibernate.

14 **What type of sentences are these?**

a I lost my mobile phone yesterday. _____

b Have you got it back? _____

c Oh, no! _____

15 **Punctuate this sentence correctly.**

When will you be here? she asked Karim.

16 **When you read a play script, what do the stage directions tell you?**

_____

17 **Match the purpose to these types of text. Draw lines to join them.**

a An entry in an encyclopedia   gives instructions

b An advertisement for a laptop   gives information

c How to mend a flat tyre   persuades

18 **Name two types of verse.**

a _____

b _____

19 **Complete this sentence.**

Predicting means using _____ in the text to _____ what might happen.

20 **Why is it important to ask yourself questions as you read a text?**

_____

How did you do?   1–5 Try again!   6–10 Good try!   **/20**

11–15 Great work!   16–20 Excellent exploring!

43

Explorer's Logbook

Tick off the topics as you complete them and then colour in the star.

How do you feel?
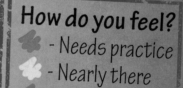
- Needs practice
- Nearly there
- Got it!

Reading aloud ☐

Supporting sentences ☐

Reading poetry ☐

Predicting ☐

Sentence types ☐

Active reading ☐

Reading play scripts ☐

Reading non-fiction ☐

Fact or opinion? ☐

Finding information ☐

Direct speech ☐

Looking at layout ☐

Vocabulary in context ☐

Summarising
the main idea ☐

Imagery ☐

Interesting words ☐

Using quotations ☐

Reading in detail ☐

Finding the main idea ☐

Looking for clues ☐

Answers

Pages 2–3

Task 1
a Kuzya   **b** Russia   **c** China

Task 2
a rescued   **b** killed   **c** trackers

Task 3
a Dr Romanov   **b** He swam across a river
c About 360   **d** About 24

Exploring Further
FIND THE DETAILS

Pages 4–5

Task 1
a something that is in nature
b quick to feel or notice
c unusual

Task 2
a if   **b** find   **c** steep   **d** clever

Task 3
Suggested answers:
a said 'no'/said he wouldn't
b annoyed
c stated /said that they were unhappy
d lazy
e replied
f tells you how/describes

Exploring Further
a survive   **b** habitats   **c** weight

Pages 6–7

Task 1
a False   **b** True   **c** False   **d** True

Task 2
a to tell us about elephant habitat
b taken over areas
c roads, railways and houses

Task 3

	Asian elephant	African elephant
ears	small	large
skin	smooth	wrinkled
back	flat	sloping
tusks	males: fairly small females: no tusks	large

Exploring Further

S	P	D	I	L	A
C	O	R	D	E	R
I	R	W	E	N	T
D	E	T	A	I	L
O	A	E	G	P	E
B	D	S	O	L	A

Pages 8–9

Task 1
a one   **b** at the beginning of a paragraph
c in a different place in the paragraph

Task 2
a In Japan, blowfish meat is considered a rare and delicious food.
b They give the reader more detail

Task 3
a The blowfish is one of the most poisonous creatures on the planet.
b There are more than 100 species of blowfish.
c blowfish poison is deadly
d types or species of blowfish

Exploring Further
a False   **b** True   **c** False

Pages 10–11

Task 1
a A large wild boar was seen in a national park in Singapore.
b boar, seen, park

Task 2
a boar, Mrs Ling, photos
b As she was cycling through the park, Mrs Ling stopped and took photos of a friendly wild boar.

Task 3
a wild boars can live near humans
b wild boars, humans, live
c **[suggested answer]** There are more wild boars in Singapore now and they are becoming used to humans.

Exploring Further
a teeth   **b** unusual   **c** Singapore
d key words   New word: TUSK

Pages 12–13

Task 1
a yes   **b** tame   **c** yes
d maybe   **e** grandad
f grandad, trapping, 'terror', pet

Task 2

Information	Clue in the text
It is hot	when it's hot
The creatures have black fur	their black fur
He knows about this creature	he explained

Task 3
a no (unwelcome)
b three (one, another, the last one)
c raining (dripping leaves)

d squirrels (nuts, leapt, huge bushy tail)

e a dog (barked)

Exploring Further

The doctor is the boy's mother.

Pages 14–15

Task 1

a cried   **b** massive   **c** delightful

d cheerfully   **e** sweltering   **f** clamorous

Task 2

Answers will vary

Task 3

a Examples: densest, spotted, scented, keen, majestic

b Accept any suitable answers using the words from part a.

Exploring Further

majestic, cried, delightful, lizard, dangerous, snake, effect

Pages 16–17

Task 1

a The Indian star tortoise has been described as 'the most beautiful tortoise in the world'.

b The phrase 'star-like' describes the pattern on their shells.

c Wildlife protection experts are calling the threat to the tortoises 'a huge tragedy'.

Task 2

a **F:** 'Three months ago'   **b** **T:** 'Is this normal?'

c **F:** 'His house is not too hot'

Task 3

a Sometimes they 'dry out too much'.

b Tariq says 'Some like it if you spray', so it may be a good idea.

Exploring Further

tortoises

Pages 18–19

Task 1

a heading   **b** image   **c** capital letters

d bold italic words   **e** bullet list

Task 2

a 3   **b** 5   **c** 4   **d** 1   **e** 2

Task 3

Answers will vary. Accept any two sentences which mention heading, list, image, colours and the effect these have on the reader.

Exploring Further

cast, acts

Pages 20–21

Task 1

a a comma – make a short pause

b a full stop – pause

c an exclamation mark – show the feeling with your voice

d a question mark – make it sound like a question

Task 2

Punctuation mark	With my voice, I ...	How did it help the meaning?
question mark	made it sound like a question	made it more interesting
exclamation mark	showed a feeling	showed surprise
comma	paused for a short time	made the meaning clearer
full stop	paused	showed the end of a sentence

Task 3

a fear

b higher, louder

c Suggested answer: scared, really (2nd one), moths, creeps, nightmare, full, flying, face, hair, ugh

Exploring Further

TROPICAL

Pages 22–23

Task 1

a M   **b** S   **c** M   **d** S

Task 2

a The eggs were as delicate as moonlight. **S**

b The beating of its wings was like soft spring rain. **S**

c She felt like a bluebird, flying free. **M**

d It holds an enchanted dream in its wings. **M**

Task 3

a like specks of daylight/simile

b butterfly blue of its wings/metaphor

c as bright as sparklers/simile

d a tiny fairy cup/metaphor

e like small clouds/simile

Exploring Further

a feather   **b** ox   **c** lead   **d** kitten

Pages 24–25

Task 1

a O   **b** O   **c** F   **d** O   **e** F

Task 2

5 from: male gaur is black/female is dark brown/ more than two metres high/horns over one metre long/travel in herds/about ten animals in each herd

Task 3

A male gaur is bigger than a bison, a buffalo or a water buffalo. Even so, gaurs are hunted by tigers, leopards and crocodiles. Tigers are awesome. It is amazing that some gaurs live so long if they are hunted by tigers. Human hunters are the other main threat to gaurs. They are hunted for their meat and their horns.

Exploring Further

ARGUE

Pages 26–27

Task 1

a A prized pet peacock was stolen last night.

b 4

Task 2

d

Task 3

a, b, d, e.

Exploring Further

a jungle **b** ant **c** petal

d peacock **e** feather

Pages 28–29

Task 1

a Command – gives an instruction

b Question – asks for an answer

c Statement – gives information

d Exclamation – expresses an emotion

Task 2

a 2 **b** 4 **c** 1 **d** 3

Task 3

Sentence type	Example
Command	Watch how he swings from side to side.
Statement	The king bird of paradise hangs upside down as part of his mating display.
Question	Do you think he feels dizzy?
Exclamation	He's a brilliant acrobat!

Exploring Further

a The bird of paradise is sometimes called 'the dancer of the jungle'./statement

b Its tail feathers are absolutely gorgeous!/exclamation

Pages 30–31

Task 1

a 'They look more like teddy bears than wild animals!' said Malia.

b He said, 'The loris can stay completely still for hours at a time.'

c 'Make a donation to save the loris's habitat!' he urged.

d 'With those thumbs,' he went on, 'they can grip the trees, just like monkeys – or humans!'

e 'They look so furry and cuddly' said Rakhee.

Task 2

The guide told us some fun facts about the loris. 'The short second finger on each foot helps it to hold on to branches,' he explained. He went on, 'Its eyes are huge and that means it can see well in the dark.' Then he told us, 'They look cute and furry but they are actually poisonous predators. They cover their teeth before they bite into their enemies!'

Task 3

Suggested answers:

a "The name loris comes from a Dutch word meaning clown.'

b 'It's because of their comical appearance, which makes them very desirable as pets.'

c 'Loris are hunted and then sold on the streets or in animal markets.'

Exploring Further

a loris **b** poisonous **c** nocturnal

Pages 32–33

Task 1

a evening; a forest trail near Poon Hill **b** 2

c first tired then scared

d Not far now! Only about two miles.

Task 2

a 3 **b** nervous, delighted

Task 3

a They change from joking to nervous and then frightened

b joking/laughing

c disappointed

Exploring Further

a colon (:) **b** no **c** stage directions

Pages 34–35

Task 1

a persuades **b** gives instructions

c gives information or facts

d explains how something works

Task 2

a World Pangolin Day

b To persuade people to support World Pangolin Day

c leaflet

d wildlife lovers

Exploring Further

c

Pages 36–37

Task 1

	Free	Formal
does not follow any rules	✓	
often sounds natural, like normal speech	✓	
usually has a regular rhythm		✓
usually rhymes		✓

Task 2

a space/face, sized/eyed, you/shrew

b formal verse

c The lines rhyme

d free verse

e Answers will vary: accept any reasonable answers. Suggested answers: